TABLE OF CONTENTS

BEST INTRO EVER!

Salutations from the Captain's chair of the Android's Dungeon, Springfield's world-renowned comic book shop and the finest purveyor of sport cards and sci-fi/fantasy collectibles in the tri-city area. (Nerts to you, Frodo's of Shelbyville!)

While recently engaged in a spirited discourse with my online role-playing group, the subject of the impending holidays reared its head. The question put before The Continuum was, in a wintertime scenario, which frost-bound character would you be? Predictably many opted for the heroic demeanor of Iceman, or the cold-hearted villainy of Mr. Freeze or even the innocuous japery of Chilly Willy. While Frink 8.5 (the fool) remained unshakable in his position that Captain Cold is a far superior evil-doer than Mr. Freeze (oh please) and The Internet King staunchly defended some nobody named Mr. Plow, I remained steadfast in my conviction that the greatest of all winter characters is the one and only Santa Claus.

Yes, I truly envy that jolly old soul. Why, his ready access to eggnog and gingerbread alone secures him the top spot in my price guide. And let us not forget his happy little helpers. Imagine, if your Muggle brain will let you, commanding legions of elf-lackeys to fashion the rarest of treasures for your personal collection. If I were blessed with the power of the Clausinator, crates of banned missile-launching Boba Fett action figures would line my workshop. I'd use Fantasia animation cels as place mats and wipe doughnut sprinkles from my mouth with Joe DiMaggio baseball cards.

Most wondrous of all, I would have my sprightly drones faithfully re-create classics of graphic storytelling long out of print. Classics like the merry tales contained herein. You hold in your unworthy hands **The Simpsons Holiday Humdinger**, a compilation of seasonal glee from our favorite family's Christmases past. Any one of these now priceless books would cost you a fortune on the back issue market, if you could find them (and rest assured you can't), but thanks to the magic of the Yuletide season, they are yours merely for the wishing, and of course, the $14.95 marked on the back cover.

Now heat up the cocoa, break out the cookies, assemble your friends (super or otherwise), and enjoy this diverting selection of holiday frippery.

And don't forget the Dungeon's Post-Xmas Clearance Sale 11 A.M. to 9 P.M. on Dec. 26th. All seasonal merchandise 40% off! (No refunds or exchanges.)

Comic Book Guy

THE SIMPSONS
HOLIDAY HUMDINGER

HarperCollins*Entertainment*
An Imprint of HarperCollinsPublishers

Dedicated to Snowball I:

As this snow sculpture thaws on the first warm day,
so will our hearts melt whenever we think of you.

The Simpsons™, created by Matt Groening, is the copyrighted
and trademarked property of Twentieth Century Fox Film Corporation.
Used with permission. All rights reserved.

THE SIMPSONS™ HOLIDAY HUMDINGER

HarperCollinsEntertainment

An imprint of HarperCollinsPublishers
77–85 Fulham Palace Road
Hammersmith, London W6 8JB
www.harpercollins.co.uk

Published by HarperCollinsEntertainment 2004
3 5 7 9 8 6 4 2

ISBN 0-00-719170-7

Printed in Great Britain by Butler & Tanner.

Publisher: Matt Groening
Creative Director: Bill Morrison
Managing Editor: Terry Delegeane
Director of Operations: Robert Zaugh
Special Projects Art Director: Serban Cristescu
Art Director: Nathan Kane
Production Manager: Christopher Ungar
Production/Design: Karen Bates, Art Villanueva
Production Assistance: Chia-Hsien Jason Ho, Mike Rote
Editorial Assistance: Sherri Smith, Nathan Hamill
Legal Guardian: Susan A. Grode

Book Concepts and Design: Serban Cristescu

Contributing Artists:
Karen Bates, Tim Bavington, John Costanza, Isabelle Cristescu, Serban Cristescu, Luis Escobar,
Stephanie Gladden, Nathan Kane, William Mahaney, Bill Morrison, Kevin M. Newman, Phil Ortiz, Mike Rote,
Howard Shum, Steve Steere Jr., Chris Ungar, Art Villanueva

Contributing Writers:
Ian Boothby, Paul Dini, Scott M. Gimple, Jason Grode, Bill Morrison, Gail Simone, Mary Trainor

HarperCollins Editors: Susan Weinberg, Kate Travers, and David Brawn (UK)

Special Thanks to:
Pete Benson, N. Vyolet Diaz, Deanna MacLellan, Mili Smythe, and Ursula Wendel

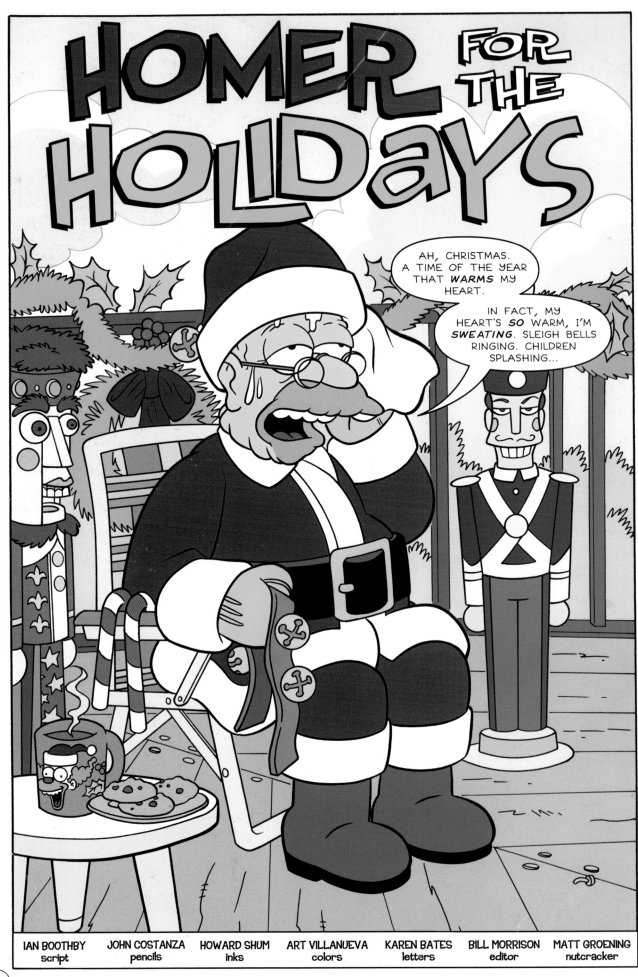

HOMER FOR THE HOLIDAYS

AH, CHRISTMAS. A TIME OF THE YEAR THAT *WARMS* MY HEART.

IN FACT, MY HEART'S *SO* WARM, I'M *SWEATING*. SLEIGH BELLS RINGING. CHILDREN SPLASHING...

IAN BOOTHBY
script

JOHN COSTANZA
pencils

HOWARD SHUM
inks

ART VILLANUEVA
colors

KAREN BATES
letters

BILL MORRISON
editor

MATT GROENING
nutcracker

9

BART THE RED-NOSED REINDEER

NORTH POLE

OKAY, LISTEN UP! THIS IS OUR *NEW REIN-DEER*, BART. NOW, I DON'T WANT ANYONE MAKING FUN OF HIS HILARIOUSLY FREAKISH *NOSE*!

GOT THAT?

GOT IT!

HERE'S YOUR BALL. HAVE FUN WITH YOUR REINDEER GAMES.

SO, WHAT ARE WE PLAYING?

MURDER BALL.

HOW DO YOU PLAY?

10 MINUTES LATER...

DID I *WIN*?

HEY LISTEN, *ROSEY LE NEZ* IS TALKING.

WHAT'S THAT *REDDY VON SCHNOZZINGTON*? YOU SAY YOU WANT SOME MORE?

20 MINUTES LATER...

MY ARMS ARE GETTING *TIRED*.

MINE TOO. WANNA GO FLYING? WE CAN BUZZ SOME *NERDS* AT THE ELF LIBRARY.

DUDE, I AM *SO* THERE!

10

LATER...

IF YOU'RE LOST, JUST *SAY* YOU'RE LOST.

NO, I'M SURE IT'S AROUND HERE.

THERE!

WHOA! LOOK AT ALL THE *TOYS!*

BART! BE CAREFUL!

BE CAREFUL OF A JACK IN THE BOX? MAN, YOU PUT THE "WUSS" IN WUSSY, LITTLE ELF!

FWOOSH!

BOING!

AAAAH!

WELCOME TO THE *LAND OF DEFECTIVE TOYS!*

OW! HEY, LOOK AT THE *TAG.* ARE *ALL* THESE TOYS MADE BY KRUSTYCO INDUSTRIES?

YEAH, WHAT ARE YA GONNA DO? THERE WERE SOME...*TROUBLES*. MY LAWYER PLEA BARGAINED ME DOWN TO *BANISHMENT* ON THIS ISLAND WITH THE TOYS.

POOR LITTLE GUYS.

ALL WE WANT IS SOME CHILD TO LOVE US AND PLAY WITH US!

OW! THOSE SHARP CLAWS! *MY EYE!*

MAYBE I COULD PUT IN A *GOOD WORD* WITH SANTA.

WOW, PARDNER! THAT'D BE *GREAT!*

BLAM!

OW! *MY LEG!*

SOON...

THANKS, MILHOUSE. I THOUGHT *I* WAS THE ONLY ONE WHO WAS DIFFERENT. BUT NOW I KNOW THAT NO MATTER HOW BAD THINGS GET...

...THAT YOU'VE GOT *FRIENDS?*

NO, I'LL ALWAYS KNOW THAT AT LEAST I'M *BETTER* THAN ALL OF YOU.

I'M GONNA SHOW SANTA THAT I'VE GOT WHAT IT TAKES! GOODBYE, EVERYONE!

GOOD LUCK, KID!

WAIT! YOU'RE MY RIDE *HOME!*

AND THAT WAS THE STORY OF THE VERY *FIRST* CHRISTMAS *EXTORTION*.

GRAMPA, SERIOUSLY, LOOK AROUND! IT'S SUMMER. YOU'RE *EMBARRASSING* ME! THIS COULDN'T GET ANY WORSE!

HOLD IT THERE, MISTER! YOU FORGOT YOUR *SUNSCREEN*!

AW, MOM!

YOU CAN'T BE TOO CAREFUL, *SPF 2000* IS THE ONLY SUN-SCREEN THAT ACTUALLY *REMOVES* THE SUN FROM YOUR SKIN.

WHITER SHADE OF PALE brand SUNSCREEN SPF 2000

HA! HA! BART'S A *SNOWMAN*!

FUNNY YOU SHOULD MENTION THAT. REMINDS ME OF A STORY...

≋SIGH≋

≋SIGH≋

FROSTEE THE SNOWMOM

THIS IS HARD WORK. I WISH WE HAD *PARENTS*.

WHAT ARE WE GOING TO CALL HIM?

WHY DOES IT HAVE TO BE A *HIM*?

YOU'RE ON YOUR OWN ORPHANAGE
A DIVISION OF BURNS
CHILD LABOR INDUSTRIES

WHO ARE YOU?

I'M FROSTEE THE SNOWMOM!

THAT'S GREAT! WE'RE ALL ORPHANS. IT'LL BE NICE TO HAVE SOMEONE TO TUCK US IN AND READ US STORIES!

THIS ORPHANAGE IS A *MESS*.

YEAH, PEOPLE USED TO COME AND CLEAN. THERE WAS AN INCIDENT WITH SOME CHERRY BOMBS, AND THEY QUIT. BUT NOW, *YOU'RE* HERE!

I'M YOUR SNOWMOM, NOT YOUR SNOW*MAID*! ALL OF YOU, GET CLEANING!

≥SIGH≤

LATER...

WE'RE DONE.

WANNA TAKE US SLEDDING?

IS YOUR HOMEWORK DONE?

I SEE THREE SPELLING MISTAKES. DO IT OVER.

BUT...

YOU'LL *THANK ME* WHEN YOU'RE OLDER.

YAY!

HEY! USE YOUR *INDOOR* VOICES!

BUT WE'RE *OUT*DOORS.

THAT *BACK-TALK* JUST EARNED *YOU* A TIME OUT!

SNOWMOM IS A *STONE COLD DRAG!*

OH, SHE'S NOT SO BAD. A LITTLE *DISCIPLINE* NEVER HURT ANYONE.

LISA, WHY ARE YOU TALKING WHEN YOU SHOULD BE PRACTICING YOUR SAXOPHONE?

BUT IT'S TOO COLD AND...

NO BUTS! GET OUT HERE AND LET ME HEAR YOU PLAY.

ONE MINUTE LATER...

DON'T WORRY, LISA. I'VE LICKED A LOT OF *WINTER METAL* IN MY TIME, AND THE SKIN *ALWAYS* GROWS BACK BY *SPRING*.

SHE'S *GOING DOWN!*

THE NEXT DAY...

WELL, I THINK I'M GOING TO GO INSIDE AND COOK MYSELF DINNER.

SOUNDS GOOD. WHAT'LL YOU MAKE?

CANDY CORN ON THE COB AND FUDGE SOUP.

YOU TWO HOLD IT *RIGHT THERE!*

LISTEN, DID YOU SEE A *MAGIC BROOM* AROUND HERE? I LOST MINE, AND THEY DON'T COME CHEAP.

ARE YOU GONNA *EAT* US?

WELL, NOW THAT YOU MENTION IT. I *AM* A BIT PECKISH. ARE CHILDREN HIGH CARB OR LOW CARB?

AND AFTER YOU'VE DONE THAT THERE'S SOME IRONING THAT...

HELP! A *WITCH* IS AFTER ME!

YAAAAH!

OH THIS IS *ALL* I NEED!

NOW YOU'RE RIPPING OFF *THE WIZARD OF OZ,* MAN!

NEVER HEARD OF IT.

IT'S A *CLASSIC.* THEY SHOW IT EVERY CHRISTMAS!

SO, IT'LL BE ON IN *SIX MONTHS!*

OH, YOU WANT SOME *CHRISTMAS CLASSICS,* DO YA?

WHEN IT'S *CHRISTMAS!*

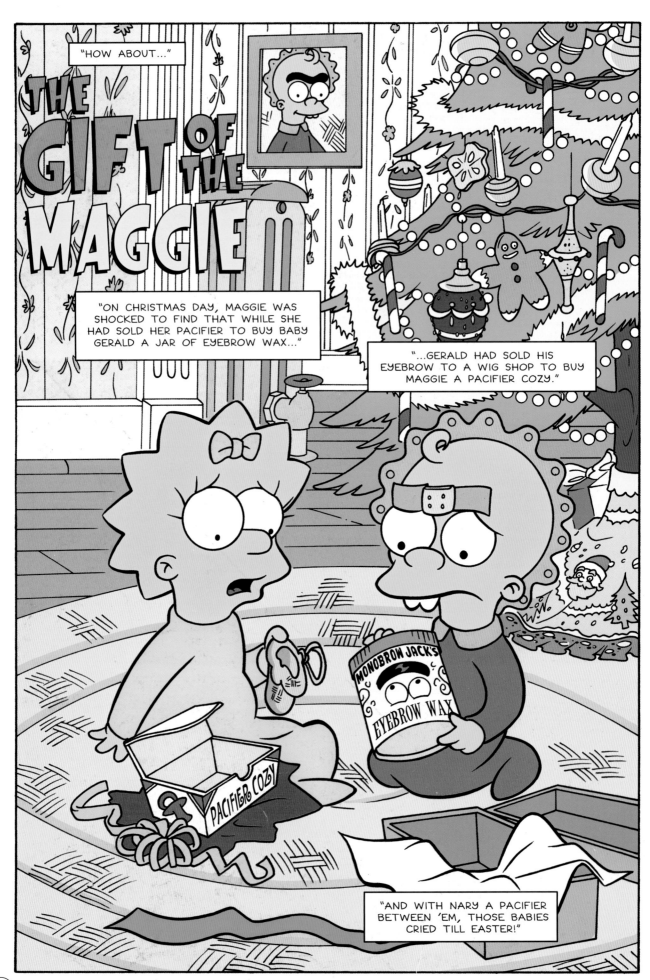

JINGLE BELLS, BARTMAN SMELLS

I CERTAINLY DO *LOVE* CHRISTMAS.

"THE FOLKS DOWN IN SPRINGFIELD LIKED CHRISTMAS A LOT."

I CONCUR!

♪ JINGLE BELLS! ♪ JINGLE BELLS! JINGLE ♪ ALL THE WAY... ♪

YAY, CHRISTMAS!

"BUT *THE GIL*, WHO LIVED IN A 20-STORY WALKUP...DID NOT."

OL' GIL JUST WANTS A LITTLE PEACE AND QUIET, BUT THEY WON'T STOP WITH THEIR SINGING AND LAUGHING AND THE OLD HO-HO-HO-ING..

"IT WAS THEN THAT GIL HAD HIMSELF AN IDEA."

I COULD FAKE MY OWN DEATH, GET A WIG AND DRESS, PRETEND TO BE MY DAUGHTER, AND COLLECT THE INSURANCE.

"IT WAS THEN THAT GIL HAD A *BETTER* IDEA."

OR...I'LL *STOP* CHRISTMAS FROM COMING.

"MEANWHILE, DOWN IN THE CITY, AS GIL THOUGHT OF HIS PLAN, GUARDING THE CITY WAS THE ONE KNOWN AS..."

BARTMAN!

YEAH, WE'D LOVE TO COME OVER AND HELP YOU OUT, BUT THE THING IS WE ALL ATE SOME *UNDER RIPE* PEARS AND...

WELL, WE SHOULD REALLY STAY BY THE LITTLE LAW ENFORCERS ROOM.

THE POLICE ARE USELESS. EVEN MORE SO THAN USUAL. HEY, *A CLUE!*

GIL PLANS TO COMMIT AN INCREDIBLE CRIME.

TIME FOR *BARTMAN* TO ACT AND TO TALK NOW IN *RHYME.*

"AND SO WHILE THE SIMPSONS WENT BACK TO THEIR BEDS..."

THAT GUY ON THE FLANDERS' ROOF IS STEALING SOMETHING OF NED'S.

AW GEEZ, WHY DO PEOPLE HAVE TO HAVE SUCH HEAVY PRESENTS? AND WHAT'S THIS BIRD THEY WERE STUFFING? GOOSE? SQUAB?

IT'S PHEASANT!

UM, HOPE YOU DON'T MIND ME ASKING, BUT WHY ARE YOU DRESSED LIKE A BUNNY?

THEY WERE ALL OUT SANTA SUITS. DOES IT LOOK FUNNY?

OL' GIL THOUGHT WRECKING THIS DAY'D BE A CINCH.

BUT IT'S HARDER THAN IT LOOKS TO ACT LIKE A GRINCH.

"I TRIED PUTTING SOME ANTLERS ON A DOG AS STEP ONE."

"BUT THE PIT BULL DIDN'T LIKE IT WHEN I USED THE GLUE GUN."

AND MY SCOOTER CAN'T HANDLE ANY MORE THAN THREE GIFTS.

THEY DON'T GIVE RABBITS LIFTS.

HOW 'BOUT A CAB?

UM...UH... Y'KNOW, DUDE, CAN WE JUST DROP THE RHYMING?

THAT'D BE A RELIEF! I JUST DON'T HAVE THE TIMING.

Y'KNOW MAYBE THIS WAS A BAD IDEA. NO ONE CAN REALLY STEAL CHRISTMAS.

MAYBE NOT, BUT WITH THE COPS INDISPOSED AND YOU DISTRACTING BARTMAN, WE ALL THOUGHT WE'D GIVE IT THE OLD COLLEGE TRY!

THEY'VE STOLEN EVERY PRESENT IN TOWN!

AW, GIL JUST HAD ONE MORE PAYMENT ON THAT SCOOTER!

CHRISTMAS MORNING...

SO WHAT HAPPENS NOW?

LOOK AT ALL THOSE PEOPLE GATHERING IN THE TOWN SQUARE, GIL.

ARE THEY SINGING?

NO...THEY'RE *LOOTING*.

SMASH!

TINKLE!

CRASH!

ARE YOU GONNA STOP THEM?

NAW, IT'S KINDA *NICE* SEEING THE WHOLE TOWN DOING SOMETHING *TOGETHER*.

MAYBE *THAT'S* WHAT CHRISTMAS IS ALL ABOUT.

MERRY CHRISTMAS, GIL.

CHEESE LOG

TO: HOMER

MAN, MY OWN *CHEESE LOG*. NOW, LOOK WHAT YOU'VE DONE. OL' GIL HAS SOMETHING IN HIS EYE.

MERRY CHRISTMAS, BARTMAN!

TREE'S COMPANY

YOU CALL THIS A NUCLEAR POWER PLANT CHRISTMAS PAGEANT? I'VE SEEN CARNIVAL DUCKS ON HOT PLATES THAT DANCED WITH MORE GRACE!

I'VE FAILED YOU, SIR. FEEL FREE TO FLOG ME WITH THIS CANDY CANE.

IT'S NOT YOU, SMITHERS. YOU'VE BREATHED *NEW LIFE* INTO THE ROLE OF *CHRISTMAS QUEEN*. BUT SOMETHING IS LACKING.

MAYBE A *TREE* WOULD HELP.

YES! HAVE FIVE ACRES OF RAINFOREST FLOWN IN, AND WE'LL PICK THE BEST OF THE LOT.

ARE YOU SURE, SIR? YOU'LL MAKE *STING* CRY.

≋WHIMPER≋

OH, VERY WELL.

YOU! THE ONE BOBBING FOR FRUIT CAKES!

HUH?

HEAVY WATER

FETCH ME THE MOST BEAUTIFUL TREE IN TOWN, OR YOU'RE *FIRED*!

CAN LENNY COME, TOO?

YES, BUT HE'LL BE FIRED, TOO.

THANKS A LOT, HOMER!

WHAT'S WITH THE *BLANKET*?

WHY?

IT MAKES ME FEEL SECURE.

I CARRY A *CROSSBOW* UNDER IT.

YOU NEVER KNOW WHEN YOU'LL MEET UP WITH A PACK OF WOLVES.

LENNY, WHAT DO YOU THINK CHRISTMAS IS ALL ABOUT?

WELL, LET'S SEE. THE WORD CHRISTMAS COMES FROM *CRISTES MAESSE* OR *CHRIST'S MASS*. WHILE MANY CULTURES IN PLACES LIKE ROME AND EUROPE ALREADY HAD A *WINTER FESTIVAL*, THE *CHRISTIAN CHURCH* ONLY CELEBRATED *EASTER*. THAT CHANGED IN THE FOURTH CENTURY. THE BIRTHDAY OF CHRIST, THOUGH NOT RECORDED IN THE BIBLE, WAS FIRST CELEBRATED AS JANUARY 6TH.

THIS CHANGED IN 1743 WHEN POPE JULIUS THE FIRST MADE THE DATE DECEMBER 25TH IN ORDER, IT'S ASSUMED, TO COINCIDE WITH THE PAGAN *SATURNALIA FESTIVAL*. FOR A TIME IN BOSTON, 1659 TO 1681, CHRISTMAS WAS OUTLAWED, BUT BY 1870 IT WAS DECLARED A *NATIONAL HOLIDAY* AND REMAINS ONE TO THIS DAY.

WHAT DO *YOU* THINK CHRISTMAS IS ALL ABOUT, HOMER?

I LIKE EGG NOG.

HERE WE ARE. MAN, LOOK AT ALL THEM TREES!

THIS ONE IS *PERFECT*.

ARE YOU NUTS? IT'S THE RUNT OF THE LITTER.

ALL IT NEEDS IS A *LITTLE LOVE*.

I DUNNO, HOMER. I HAVE A HARD ENOUGH TIME TELLING MY *MA* I LOVE HER.

IT'S GONNA BE EVEN HARDER SAYING IT TO A *TWIG*.

WE'LL **TAKE** IT.

AW NUTS! WHERE DID I LEAVE MY BLANKET?

DON'T WORRY ABOUT IT, WE'LL JUST...

YAAAAA!

WOLVES!

A SHORT TIME AND ONE MAULING LATER...

GEEZ, I DUNNO, HOMER.

SIMPSON, WHAT IS THIS? SOME KIND OF *JOKE*?!

IT JUST NEEDS SOME WATER.

HOMER, THAT AIN'T REGULAR WATER! IT'S RADIO-ACTIVE!

HEAV

WHAT'S GOING ON IN HERE? ⊰GASP!⊱ THAT *TREE!* IT'S *PERFECT!*

SPRONG!

"WAIT A MINUTE!"

32

33

Angry Dad in "Wreck the Halls"
by Bart Simpson

KWIK HOLIDAY

Ol' St. Nahasapeemapetilon SAYS:

Forget to make those all-important gift purchases for the holidays? Afraid of spending Christmas Day in the house of the dog?

Well, do not worry, my non-Hindu friend! We have the answers at the...

YOU SAY YOU FORGOT TO PURCHASE SMALL ITEMS FOR THE TRADITIONAL STUFFING OF OVERSIZED FOOTWEAR?

NOT TO BE WORRIED! CHOOSE FROM A SANTA-SIZED SELECTION OF PENCILS, TAPE, OINTMENTS, GAUZES, EYE DROPS, TISSUES, CONDIMENT PACKAGES, SWABS, SEALANTS, LIGHTERS, BUG SPRAYS, FLU REMEDIES, BATTERIES, RAZORS, LUBRICATING JELLIES, TICK POWDERS, AND A FESTIVE ARRAY OF LUNCHEON MEATS AND HEAD CHEESES!

WITH ALL THE HOLIDAY HUSTLE AND ALSO BUSTLE, CAN A FATHER NOT BE FORGIVEN FOR FORGETTING TO PURCHASE A CHARMING CENTERPIECE FROM A HEARTLESS DEPARTMENT STORE?

NEVER FEAR! NOTHING SAYS "I LOVE MY FAMILY" LIKE A DICKENS VILLAGE MADE TOTALLY OF JERKY!

DO NOT WORRY ABOUT *THE BEEF* BEING INFECTED WITH THE MADNES OF COWS. THERE *IS* NO BEE IT HAS BEEN REPLACED BY EXTRA SULPHIDES AND SOME WOOD PULP!

AS A MOM, I *LIKE* THAT!

Last minute elegance that the dog will clean up FOR you!

The kids will squeal (with joy)!

MANY IS THE HARD-WORKING HUSBAND WHO NEGLECTED TO PURCHASE A GIFT FOR HIS LOVELY BRIDE. THE ANSWER? *CANDY JEWELRY,* AT A *FRACTION* OF THE PRICE OF THE REAL THING!

She'll be delighted and sticky!

ZIP!

FWOOOOSH!

YAAAAAAHH!!

PAT PAT PAT PAT PAT PAT PAT

TUG!
TUG!

BONK!

BOMP!

KRIK!
KRIK!
KRIK!

FWIT!

FWAT!

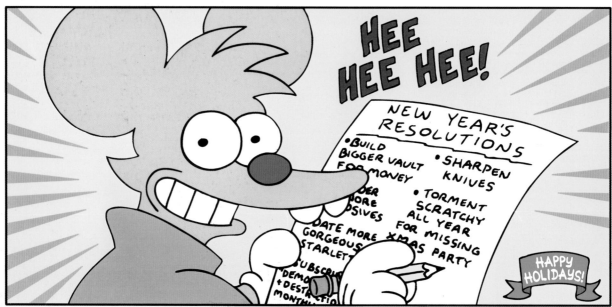

G reetings, lucky friends, family, patients, former patients, future patients, gauze suppliers, pharmaceutical junket coordinators, nosy mailmen, and Consuela, the best housekeeper in Springfield! Just why are you so lucky? Well, you have just received...

DR. JULIUS HIBBERT'S FAMILY PRACTICE KWANZAA LETTER!

> FOR THOSE OF YOU WHO AREN'T FAMILIAR WITH THE HOLIDAY, *KWANZAA* IS A UNIQUE AFRICAN-AMERICAN CELEBRATION WITH A FOCUS ON THE TRADITIONAL AFRICAN VALUES OF FAMILY, COMMUNITY RESPONSIBILITY, COMMERCE, AND SELF-IMPROVEMENT.

> FOR THOSE OF YOU WHO AREN'T FAMILIAR WITH *ME*, I'M THE DOCTOR WITH THE DULCIMER GIGGLE WHO'D LIKE TO REMOVE THAT GROWTH FROM YOUR BACK!

> KWANZAA LASTS *SEVEN GLORIOUS DAYS*, WITH EACH DAY A FOCUS ON ONE OF THE *NGUZO SABA*! THAT'S NOT KLINGON, FRIENDS--THAT'S *SWAHILI!* THE *NGUZO SABA* ARE THE SEVEN PRINCIPLES OF KWANZAA. WHAT *ARE* THESE SEVEN PRINCIPLES, AND HOW IS YOUR PAL DOCTOR HIBBERT *FULFILLING* THEM THIS HOLIDAY SEASON? *READ ON!*

Umoja (Unity)

The first principle of Kwanzaa is to strive for and maintain **unity**. In the spirit of this day, I got **Krusty the Clown** to finally make amends with his estranged sidekick, **Sideshow Raheem**. They're currently in development on what's sure to be a hilarious new UPN sitcom called "**Clizzy in Da Hizzy.**"

ujichagulia (Self-Determination)

e second principle of Kwanzaa is **self-determination.** On Day Two, etermined that I'd rather play golf than work at the Springfield ot Clinic.

jima (Collective Work and Responsibility)

e principle of **Ujima** is about making our fellow man's problems r own, and to solve them **together**. That's why I held "Free Mole noval Day" at the Springfield Mall on Day Three.

HACK-A-MOLE!

THE DOCTOR IS IN

Doc Hibbert's GOOD-TIME SWEATER EXPERIENCE

Ujamaa (Cooperative Economics)

Ujamaa encourages African-Americans to open our own stores and to patronize them. That's why I finally fulfilled my lifelong dream of opening a first-class sweaterteria. Like what you see? That's Alpaca hair, purchased from my cousin's herd! The tags were sewn by a fraternity at Grambling State! Cornell West designed our new collection of turtlenecks! See, we scratch each other's back, and I mean **literally**! Some of these babies are 100% wool!

Nia (Purpose)

The fifth day of Kwanzaa has to do with **setting personal goals**—and recognizing how they fit into the community. That's why I'm involving elderly Springfielders in my weight training program. Right now, I'm up to twenty reps of Hans Moleman. This time next month, I hope to be doing dead lifts of Abraham Simpson, who, thanks to my biweekly efforts in the emergency room, continues to be very much alive.

Kumba (Creativity)

Day Six of Kwanzaa celebrates **Kumba**, or **creativity**. To celebrate, I baked the family a sweet potato pie in the shape of Africa, which I served à la Mode-agascar.

I HAVE A DREAM (THAT YOU'LL HELP WASH THE DISHES!)

Imani (Faith)

Imani is about ascending to a new level of greatness for our people and all humankind by **believing** in ourselves, both individually and as a whole. It is **faith** that is the focus of this final day of Kwanzaa. So I challenged Iron Chef Japanese to a duel while removing Jasper's gallbladder **blindfolded**!

Kwanzaa Yenu Iwe Na Heri! (May your Kwanzaa be one of Happiness, Prosperity, and Goodness!) To that end, please take this coupon, with my compliments and Kwanzaa blessings!

HAPPY HOLIDAYS!

Good for one **FREE** OBJECT EXTRACTION*, DECORATIVE WOUND STITCH**, or CAUTERIZATION!

EXPIRES: St. Patrick's Day, 2005.

*Extracted objects become the property of Dr. Julius Hibbert M.D.
**Choices include skull, Pac-Man, "Kilroy was here" cartoon, dollar sign, and Van Halen symbol. Other designs require upgrade.

SANTA'S TOY SHOP

FA, LA, LA, LA, LAAA, LA, LA, LA, LAAA!

THANKS FOR COMING IN, ABE. AS YOU'RE THE *BEST WRITER* TO EVER GRACE THIS MISERABLE *HACK-HOUSE*, I'M HOPING YOU CAN HELP ME OUT OF A JAM.

DO I *KNOW* YOU?

ROGER MEYERS JR.

HA, HA! OH, HOW I'VE MISSED THE *RAZOR-SHARP WIT* THAT SCRIPTED THOSE *PRIZE-WINNING* "ITCHY AND SCRATCHY" CARTOONS!

HEY, *WE* WERE THE ONES WHO WROTE... OWW!

HEH, HEH! DON'T BE *SILLY*, BART! MR. MEYERS DOESN'T PAY *KIDS* TO WRITE CARTOONS!

OOH, THAT'S RIGHT!

Y'SEE, ABE, THE NETWORK'S GOTTEN *TIRED* OF RUNNING *"THE HAPPY LITTLE ELVES SAVE CHRISTMAS"* *THIRTY-FIVE YEARS* IN A ROW.

THEY WANT A *NEW HOLIDAY SPECIAL*, AND I NEED YOU TO COME UP WITH SOMETHING *FRESH*. SOMETHING BRILLIANT. *SOMETHING SIMPSON!*

The Happy Little Elves Save Christmas!

I'M *DEPENDING* ON YOU, ABE.

REST ASSURED, MR. CARTOON-MAN. I'LL DEVOTE MY *EVERY WAKING HOUR* TO YOUR PROBLEM.

ROGER MEYERS JR.

EIGHTEEN SECONDS LATER...

I'M THINKING SOMETHING *CLASSICAL*, LIKE *DICKENS!*

ZZZZAWW....

DON'T FORGET, HE ALSO WANTED SOMETHING *UNIQUELY* SIMPSON.

HOW'S THIS?

COOL! I THINK IT'S TIME TO BRING THE *STORYBOARD ARTISTS* IN ON THIS. WE'LL CALL IT...

A Springfield Christmas Carol

Written by
Abraham Simpson
and Company

"WE START AT THE SPRINGFIELD NUCLEAR POWER PLANT, WHERE THE POOR, DOWNTRODDEN *WORKERS* ARE *SLAVING AWAY* THROUGH THE CHRISTMAS HOLIDAYS."

"MEANWHILE, THE PLANT'S *STINGY OWNER*, C. MONTGOMERY SCROOGE, SITS AT HIS DESK, DOING WHAT ALL *MISERS* DO THIS TIME OF THE YEAR."

BAH, HUMBUG! THE ONLY THING *GOOD* ABOUT CHRISTMAS IS THAT PEOPLE STAY HOME AND TURN UP THE *HEAT*.

C. MONTGOMERY SCROOGE

"AND DOWN IN THE BOWELS OF THE PLANT, WE FIND OUR *HERO*, POOR, OVERWORKED HOMER CRATCHIT."

SECTOR 7-G

"BUT ON THIS *SPECIAL NIGHT*, HE IS VISITED BY THAT *MAGICAL LITTLE MAN* ONLY *HE* CAN SEE."

WHY ARE YOU STILL HERE, D'OH-D'OH? IT'S *CHRISTMAS EVE*. SHOULDN'T YOU BE HOME WITH THE WIFE AND HOUSE-APES?

OH, GREAT *OZMODIAR*! THAT MEAN MONTGOMERY SCROOGE IS FORCING US TO WORK THROUGH THE *HOLIDAYS*!

IF ONLY THERE WAS SOME WAY TO *REKINDLE* THE *MAGIC OF CHRISTMAS* IN HIS *STONY OLD HEART*.

HMMM, THERE MIGHT BE AT THAT.

"AND SO IT CAME TO PASS THAT THERE WAS *PEACE ON EARTH* THAT BRIGHT CHRISTMAS MORNING, BUT AT WHAT COST? *AT WHAT COST?!?*"

The End

KABOOM!

WOW, ABE, I DON'T KNOW *WHAT* TO SAY. THIS IS...I MEAN...WOW...

I'M SURE WHAT MR. MEYERS MEANS IS THIS SCRIPT COULD WIN GRAMPA HIS *SECOND* CARTOON AWARD.

AW, GRAMPA'S NOT IN THIS BUSINESS FOR *AWARDS*,

JUST CHECKS MADE OUT TO "CASH," PLEASE.

ZZZAWW...

COMES THE MIDDLE OF DECEMBER...

TONIGHT'S THE *BIG NIGHT!*

OUR CHRISTMAS SPECIAL'S ON!

THIS EVENING, WE ARE PLEASED TO PRESENT A *HOLIDAY EVENT* FOR THE WHOLE FAMILY...

...THE THIRTY-*SIXTH* ANNUAL SHOW-ING OF *"THE HAPPY LITTLE ELVES SAVE CHRISTMAS!"*

HEY!

WHERE'S *OUR* SPECIAL?

TYPICAL! THE NETWORKS COULDN'T STAND THE IDEA THAT KIDS MIGHT SEE SOME *QUALITY ENTERTAINMENT* FOR ONCE SO THEY STUCK THIS ON *AGAIN!*

HEY! KEEP IT DOWN! I HAVE *NO IDEA* WHAT I'M LOOKING AT...

...BUT THIS JUST MIGHT BE THE *BEST CARTOON* I EVER *WROTE!*

D'OH!

THE END

85

HEY, MAN! WHAT HAPPENED TO THE ELECTRICITY?

AAAA-AAAAH!

NO TV!!! CHRISTMAS IS RUINED!

AH, WHAT ARE YOU ALL BELLY-ACHING ABOUT? WHY, NERTZ, BACK IN MY DAY WE DIDN'T EVEN HAVE TV!

≷GASP!≶

OH MY GOSH!

THAT'S RIGHT! OL' SATAN HADN'T GOT AROUND TO IN-VENTING IT YET!

IMAGINE THAT! CHRISTMAS WITHOUT TELEVISION!

OOOOOOOOHHHHHHH!

:SHUDDER:

SO TELL US, GRAMPA, WHAT WAS IT LIKE BACK THEN?

YEAH, GRAMPA.... TELL US ABOUT WHEN *YOU* WERE A KID!

YES, GRAMPA. I THINK THE CHILDREN SHOULD HEAR HOW LIFE WAS *BEFORE* TELEVISION.

BEFORE TV STOLE OUR SOULS AWAY FROM US, YOU MEAN! *DEVILVISION,* I CALL IT! EXCEPT FOR MATLOCK, OF COURSE. MARK MY WORDS, WE'LL HAVE *BEELZEBUB* TO PAY FOR THIS...

YEAH, YEAH, GRAMPS... WE'RE ALL GONNA BURN IN HELL FOR WATCHING *TOP COPS!* WE GET THE PICTURE. NOW TELL US ABOUT WHEN YOU WERE A KID.

WELL, ALRIGHT THEN...

LET'S SEE, NOW, THERE WAS...

...ME, ABE BOY.

MY DADDY, ABE SIMPSON.

MY MOMMA, OLIDIA.

OUR OLDEST SISTER, RUBE ELLA.

MY BROTHERS, LUKE...

...AND JASON.

MY OTHER SISTERS, TORI-MAE...

...AND LISA MARIE.

BABY LEROY.

GRAMPA ZEKE...

...AND GRANDMA ZZA-ZZA.

94

OUR FAMILY'S MODEST INCOME CAME FROM A *SAW MILL* THAT MY DADDY RAN WITH *GRAMPA ZEKE*...

LOOK OUT, YOU DERN *FOOL!* YOU'RE GONNA CUT OFF YOUR...

D'OH!!!

OURS WAS A LARGE BUT CLOSE-KNIT AND LOVING FAMILY...

LANDSAKES! I WISH THEY'D INVENT SOMETHING TO KEEP KIDS SITTING IN ONE PLACE...MAYBE SOME KIND OF *BOX* THAT *LIGHTS UP,* YOU KNOW... AND MAKES *SOUNDS*...

MOMMA, YOU'RE BABBLING. ARE YOU HAVING ONE OF YOUR *SPELLS*? YOU WANT ME TO FETCH YOUR *RE-LAXING MEDICINE*?

XXX

MOMMA HAD HER HANDS FULL WITH ALL THOSE YOUNG-'UNS, BUT SHE COULD ALWAYS TURN TO *GRANDMA ZZA-ZZA* FOR SUPPORT...

DAHLINK, *REALLY!* I'D *LUFF* TO HELP YOU OUT, BUT ALL YOUR ZILLY LITTLE CHILDREN ARE CHUST TOO, TOO *BORING!*

I REMEMBER IN PARTICULAR THIS ONE YEAR. IT WAS *CHRISTMAS EVE* AND MY DADDY HAD GONE WAY UP ON SIMPSONS MOUNTAIN TO FETCH US BACK A *CHRISTMAS TREE!*

OH, NINETY-NINE BOTTLES OF BEER ON THE WALL, NINETY-NINE BOTTLES OF BEER...

HE HAD LEFT EARLY THE DAY BEFORE AND HADN'T COME BACK YET...

VAIT! ABE! I NEED NEW *PEDALS* FOR MY *EXERCYCLE!* DO BE A DAHLINK AND ZTOP ON YOUR WAY AND GET ME SOME, WON'T YOU?

YOU KNOW, GRANDPA, THIS SOUNDS *AWFULLY* FAMILIAR. DIDN'T WE SEE THIS ON *TV?*

GREAT BALD-HEADED *JUPITER!* I *TOLD* YOU, THIS WAS *BEFORE TV!*

WELL, IF IT WAS *BEFORE* TV, HOW COME YOUR FAMILY HAD *OPENING CREDITS?*

WILL YOU SHUT UP AND LET ME FINISH...

LIKE I WAS SAYING, MY DADDY AIN'T BEEN BACK YET, AND MOMMA WAS PRETTY NEAR SICK WITH WORRY...

GREG, YOU'RE THE *OLDEST*...

I'M *ABE BOY*, MOMMA.

DON'T SASS ME, BOY! I WANT YOU TO GO OUT AND FETCH YOUR DADDY BACK, YOU HEAR?

I WILL, MOMMA.

C'MON KIDS - I MADE FISH-STIX AND JELL-O. GET 'EM WHILE THEY'RE *TEPID!*

OOOOOOOH! MY *NOSE!!!*

DOINK!

I COULD *SWEAR* I SAW THIS ON *TV!*

DRAT-THE-CAT, SON! I KEEP *TELLING* YOU; THIS WAS *BEFORE TV!*

SAY, DID YOUR FAMILY HAVE A *TALKING HORSE?*

LET GRAMPA TELL HIS STORY!

GO ON, GRAMPA.

AND SO, I SET OFF TO FIND MY DADDY. I PASSED THE HOME OF THE ECCENTRIC *BALDWIN SISTERS*...

TRUDGE TRUDGE
TRUDGE TRUDGE

LOOK, IT'S THAT WHITE TRASH *ABE-BOY SIMPSON*. EVERY *CHRISTMAS EVE* HIS DADDY GOES OFF ON A BENDER AND *OLIDIA* SENDS THAT FOOL KID OUT LOOKING FOR HIM.

GOODNESS GRACIOUS. PEOPLE LIKE THAT GIVE *DRINKING* A BAD NAME.

YES, SISTER. THAT'S WHY WE MUST TAKE CARE TO SHARE OUR "RECIPE" WITH ONLY THE FINER FOLKS IN THIS TOWN...

...THE ONES WITH THE CHARM AND BREEDING TO BE ALCOHOLICS...NOT MERE DRUNKARDS!

OH, AND LOOK, SISTER. HERE COMES OUR OWN *REVEREND REED*!

LET'S GET OUT THE GOOD CRYSTAL 8-OUNCE TUMBLERS, SHALL WE?

DURING *THE GREAT DEPRESSION*, MOMMA AND THE CHILDREN WERE SOMETIMES ABLE TO *SUPPLEMENT* OUR FAMILY'S MODEST *INCOME* BY TOURING THE COUNTRY *LIP-SYNCHING* INSIPID, *WHITE-BREAD* ROCK MUSIC.

PUTTA- PUTTA- PUT!

I KNEW MOMMA WAS COUNTING ON ME AND THAT RESPONSIBILITY BEGAN TO WEIGH HEAVY ON MY SPIRITS.

VRRROOOM!

EL ABE-O

ABE, MY MAN! WHY SO GLUM, BRO?

HEY, *JASON*, *LUKE* AND *TORI-MAE!* MOMMA SENT ME OUT TO FETCH DADDY BACK, AND I CAN'T FIND HIM!

OH, MAN. I *FEEL* YOUR *PAIN.*

LUKE, LIKE, *TOTALLY* KNOWS WHAT PAIN *IS*.

WELL, CHECK IT OUT, *ABE-STER.* WE'RE MEETING *BRENDA* AND *KELLY-SUE* AT THE *TAR PIT*. WANNA HANG WITH US?

GEE, I'D LIKE TO, BUT I CAN'T LET MOMMA DOWN. THAT WOULD BREAK HER HEART.

HEAR YOU, DUDE. I FEEL MOMMA'S PAIN, *TOO!*

LUKE IS THE *KING* OF PAIN.

HE IS THE *ANGST-A-GANGSTA!* MY MAIN MAN!

WELL, I GOTTA GET GOING, GUYS. IF I DON'T FIND DADDY SOON THERE'LL BE NO CHRISTMAS ON SIMPSONS MOUNTAIN.

OH, MAN. *NO CHRISTMAS!* I AM IN *SO* MUCH *PAIN!*

FWAP!

OOOPS, SORRY, LUKE! I DIDN'T MEAN TO *UPSET* YOU!

OH, WOW! I'M GONNA GO HOME AND GET DRUNK AND MOPE AROUND AND GET OUT MY GUN AND SHOOT OUT MY STEREO AND THEN BREAK UP WITH MY GIRLFRIEND AND GIVE MYSELF A NEAR-LETHAL DOSE OF TRIPLE EXPRESSO CAFÉ LATTÉ AND MOPE AROUND SOME MORE AND THEN DRIVE MY VINTAGE PORSCHE SPEEDSTER OFF OF A CLIFF, MAN!

OOOOH! SOUNDS, LIKE, *UTTERLY TRAGIC,* LUKE. BUT CAN YOU, LIKE DROP US OFF AT THE TAR PIT FIRST?

HEY, NO PROBLEM.

VRRROOOM!

MAN, I KNOW WE'RE IN THE MIDDLE OF *THE GREAT DEPRESSION,* BUT THAT GUY IS *REALLY* DEPRESSING!

FEELING IN NEED OF A TONIC TO LIFT MY SPIRITS, I STOPPED INTO *IKE GODFREY'S* GENERAL STORE FOR A ROOT BEER...

UH, HELLO, IKE...BOY, YOU SURE HAVE *CHANGED* THE OLD PLACE!

YES. YES. YOU *BET!* I AM THOROUGHLY *MODERNIZED* NOW!

HI DIDDLY HO, BART!

MY NAME IS *ABE-BOY*, SIR.

NOW, NOW, SON. RESPECT YOUR ELDERS.

WOULD YOU CARE TO AVAIL YOURSELF OF OUR NEW SQUISHEE MACHINE?

ALTHOUGH IKE'S REMODELING HAD MADE THE STORE UNRECOGNIZABLE TO ME, AND HIS PRICES WERE ASTRONOMICALLY *HIGH* FOR 1937, I FELT ODDLY AT HOME IN THESE STRANGE SURROUNDINGS.

SLURP!

...ONE MINI-BAG PORK RINDS, $1.29; ONE SIX-PAK DUFF BEER, $3.25; TWO FROZEN CORN-DOG COMBO MEALS, $6.95...

HAVE A NICE DAY!

?

THAT'S TOTALLY UNBELIEVABLE, GRAMPA. BUT AT *LEAST* IT DOESN'T SOUND LIKE SOMETHING I'VE SEEN ON *TV!*

I DON'T KNOW WHAT WAS IN THAT SQUISHEE, BUT SUDDENLY, ALL THE COLOR DRAINED FROM MY VISION.

THEODORE!

THEODORE...*BEAVER!* YOU ANSWER ME WHEN I CALL YOU, YOUNG MAN!

BUT, I'M *ABE-BOY,* MOMMA!

JEEPERS, BEAV! DON'T TALK BACK TO MOM! YOU WANNA GET *CLOBBERED?*

IT'S ALL RIGHT, WALLY... NOW, BEAVER, YOU RUN ALONG AND FIND YOUR FATHER. I HAVE MILK AND COOKIES WAITING FOR YOU AT HOME, DEAR.

YES, MOMMA.

GOLLY, MOM. HE CAN BE SUCH A LITTLE *CREEP* SOMETIMES!

NOW, WALLY...

HOLD IT, GRAMPA! THESE *RE-RUNS* ARE BAD ENOUGH, BUT DO WE HAVE TO HAVE 'EM IN *BLACK AND WHITE?!*

THE BOY'S GOT A POINT THERE. COULDN'T YOU AT LEAST *COLORIZE* 'EM LIKE THAT *TED FONDA* GUY DOES?

THAT'S *TED TURNER,* DAD!

WILL ALL OF YOU BE QUIET AND LET GRAMPA FINISH HIS STORY?

OKAY, BUT IN COLOR, MAN.

I HAD BEGUN TO DESPAIR OF *EVER* FINDING MY DADDY.

AND THEN I SAW A LONE FIGURE STANDING ON A BRIDGE

PLEASE, *LORD*... I'M SORRY THAT I'D WISHED I'D NEVER BEEN BORN. CLARENCE, *HELP ME!* GET ME *BACK*. I DON'T CARE WHAT HAPPENS TO ME. ONLY GET ME BACK TO MY WIFE AND KIDS! I WANT TO *LIVE* AGAIN!

DADDY? MOMMA SAYS SHE WANTS YOU HOME!

NOW GET OUT OF HERE, BERT, OR I'LL HIT YOU AGAIN! GET OUT.....WHAT? *ABE BOY?* YOU *KNOW* ME, BOY? YOU KNOW WHO I *AM?!*

ZZA-ZZA'S PEDALS! ZZA-ZZA'S...THEY'RE HERE, BERT! WHAT DO YOU KNOW ABOUT THAT! *MERRY CHRISTMAS!*

MOMMA SAYS I'M TO FETCH YOU BACK, DADDY.

WOO-HOO!!!

MERRY CHRISTMAS, SIMPSONS MOUNTAIN! *MERRY CHRISTMAS,* YOU WONDERFUL OL' MOUNTAIN!

OH, GIMME A *BREAK,* GRAMPA! I'VE SEEN *THAT* ON TV A *MILLION TIMES!!*

SHUT UP, BART!!!

=SIGH=

AACH! AACH!

OH, MY, *LOOK* AT US! THE PERFECT PICTURE OF A *FAMILY* AT *HOME* ON A WINTER'S EVE!

AT THE RISK OF SOUNDING LIKE A *LUDDITE*... OR WORSE, THE *UNABOMBER*...ONE CAN'T HELP BUT FEEL THAT TECHNOLOGY AND THE ENTERTAINMENT INDUSTRY HAVE SOMEHOW DEADENED OUR *SOULS*, SQUELCHED OUR *HUMANITY*...

YEAH, AND THEY'VE HOT-WIRED GRAMPA'S *MEMORY*, TOO!

IT'S THE WORK OF *SATAN*, I TELL YOU.

WELL, *WE'LL* SHOW 'EM! WE CAN BE A FAMILY *WITHOUT* THIS STUPID BOX! I SAY WE JUST TAKE THAT TV AND *HEAVE* IT RIGHT OUT THE WINDOW!

GARRRRUMPH!

LOUSY, NO-GOOD, STINKING...

WOOOSH!

HUMMMMMMMMM

HUH?

FOOP

AAAHH...

AW, SHAZBOT!

...SO, JESUS, WHAT DO YOU WANT TO DO FOR SUPPER?

DU-UH. I DUNNO, JUDAS. WHADDA *YOUSE* GUYS WANNA DO?

THE END

Bart Simpson in... CON-NUKAH!

SAY, WEINSTEIN... WHERE'D YOU GET THAT BOSS NEW BIKE?

YEAH! YOUR BIRTHDAY WAS *LAST* MONTH! I KNOW BECAUSE I WASN'T INVITED TO YOUR PARTY, AND THE CUTS FROM THE THORN BUSHES BENEATH YOUR LIVING ROOM WINDOW STILL HAVEN'T HEALED.

OH YEAH, THAT WAS A GREAT PARTY. ALTHOUGH, ONE COULD SAY THE HELICOPTER RIDES WERE A BIT MUCH...

...ANYWAY, CHRISTMAS ISN'T FOR TWO WEEKS. WHERE'D YOU GET THE WHEELS?

WELL, I'M *JEWISH*, AND LAST NIGHT WAS THE FIRST NIGHT OF *CHANUKAH*.

FIRST NIGHT? HOW MANY *ARE* THERE?

EIGHT.

AND *EIGHT PRESENTS*?! GEEZ, YOU HAVE THE BEST SANDWICHES AT LUNCH, YOU USE WORDS LIKE "PLOTZ" WITH IMPUNITY, *AND* YOU GOT OFF FROM SCHOOL ON ROSH HASHANAH, YOM KIPPUR, AND WHEN YOUR AUNT RIVKA DIED!

THAT *TEARS* IT! I'M GETTIN' JEWY WIT' IT, *PRONTO!*

SOON...

AFTER ALL THESE YEARS, HOW COULD YOU TURN YOUR BACK ON...

MARGE, WHAT RELIGION ARE WE AGAIN?

BART, WHY DO YOU WANT TO BE JEWISH?

I HAVE COME TO THIS DECISION AFTER MUCH DISCUSSION WITH MY *TOP ADVISORS*, INCLUDING MILHOUSE AND LENNY. I BELIEVE THIS CHANGE IS CRITICAL TO MY *SPIRITUAL WELL-BEING* AND *GROWTH*.

SINCE YOU WEREN'T PREPARED, I WILL ACCEPT THE PRESENTS YOU ALL OWE ME FOR THIS SECOND NIGHT OF CHANUKAH TOMORROW. I'M A *MENSCH* THAT WAY.

OH GOD, THANK YOU, BART!

BUT ARE YOU SURE YOU WANT TO ABANDON THE FAITH YOU HAPPENED TO BE BORN INTO?

WELL, I'D RATHER BE ON KRUSTY'S TEAM THAN THE FLANDERSES'.

HMMM... THE BOY HAS A POINT THERE.

HRMMM...

THE THIRD DAY OF CHANUKAH.

BUT YOU GET BART SIMPSON! *THE* BART SIMPSON! I MEAN, IMAGINE IF *BART SIMPSON* WAS *JEWISH*! I'D BE A TRASH-TALKIN' SPIKY-HAIRED SEINFELD WITH A *FOX ATTITUDE*!

THAT, I DON'T NEED!

SLAM!

OY!

HI, BART!

LISA! WHAT ARE YOU DOING IN THAT BUSH?

I WAS FOLLOWING YOU TO SEE IF YOU WERE BEING HONEST ABOUT YOUR SPIRITUAL AWAKENING.

DID YOU SEE *THAT*?

IT'S TRADITION. A RABBI OFTEN TURNS AWAY A POTENTIAL CONVERT *THREE TIMES* TO MAKE SURE THEY'RE REALLY *SERIOUS* ABOUT IT.

OH, IT'S LIKE HOW THEY MAKE YOU SIGN A WAIVER IF YOU WANT TO GET THE "HA-HA-HOT WINGS" AT *T.G.I. KRUSTY'S*!

YES, IT'S *EXACTLY* LIKE THAT.

SHORTLY AFTER SUNDOWN...

WHOA, MAMA! "THE ITCHY AND SCRATCHY LUMBER MILL INTERACTIVE PLAYSET" WITH *LUMBERJACK SCRATCHY* AND *EARTH FIRST ITCHY*!

ITCHY and Scratchy PLAYSET

THERE ARE FIVE MORE SETS...COLLECT THEM ALL! AND YOU *WILL*, BECAUSE YOU HAVE FIVE MORE DAYS OF CHANUKAH AND MORE IMPORTANTLY, I HAVE *COUPONS*!

THE FOURTH DAY OF CHANUKAH.

BUT I WANT TO BE *JEWISH!*

EH, YOU WOULDN'T LIKE IT SO MUCH. JUDAISM IS LIKE OPERA, THE LINCOLN DOUGLAS DEBATES, AND THE ATKINS DIET, ALL ROLLED INTO *ONE!*

SAY, SHOULDN'T YOU BE IN *SCHOOL?*

WELL, WITH MY RECENT DECISION TO GO SEMITIC, PRINCIPAL SKINNER PUT ME IN CHARGE OF THE *CHANUKAH PAGEANT.* I'M GOING TO YOUR SON KRUSTY'S STUDIO TO RESEARCH *JEWISH SHOWMANSHIP.*

HEY, HEY, KIDS! IT'S THE *FOURTH DAY* OF *CHANUKAH!* EVEN THOUGH IT ISN'T QUITE SUNDOWN, LET'S LIGHT THE...

...SIDESHOW *MEL-NORAH!*

YAAAA AAAAA AAY!!!

THAT NIGHT...

BART, I'M SO PROUD OF YOUR SPIRITUAL RE--WELL, UH, YOUR *AWAKENING,* THAT I GOT YOU THIS GIFT.

OY, LIS, YOU'RE TOO MUCH.

LOOK, IT'S *A TREASURY OF JEWISH HISTORY, HUMOR, AND FOOD-ORIENTED YIDDISH PHRASES!* IT'LL HELP YOU PREPARE FOR THE BIG *CHANUKAH PAGEANT!*

OH, YEAH... THANKS, LISA. THIS IS GOING TO COME IN *REAL HANDY.*

A TREASURY OF JEWISH HISTORY, HUMOR AND FOOD-ORIENTED YIDDISH PHRASES!

THE FIFTH DAY OF CHANUKAH.

BART! YOU WERE SUPPOSED TO USE THAT BOOK TO PREPARE FOR THE PAGEANT, NOT AS A *TV TRAY!*

I'LL HAVE YOU KNOW IT'S HOLDING MY *DR. BROWN'S CREAM SODA* AND A BOWL OF LO-CARB *HAMENTASHEN.*

WELL, MOM SAYS YOU HAVE *CHORES* TO DO!

I'M AFRAID THAT'S AGAINST MY *RELIGION.*

OH C'MON, BART! YOU DON'T EXPECT ME TO BELIEVE...

PAGE 18.

SOON...

BART, I'M SO SORRY. I DIDN'T REALIZE THAT YOU'RE OBSERVING SHABBAT, THE JEWISH *SABBATH* ON WHICH NO JEW SHOULD WORK.

GEEZ, I'M SORRY I CAN'T HELP WITH CHORES, BUT...WELL...YOU KNOW...*GOD.*

IT'S SUCH AN INSPIRATION TO SEE ANOTHER SIMPSON DARING TO BE DIFFERENT.

MOM! THE *LIMITED EDITION HONG KONG POOCHIE DOLL!* YOU REMEMBERED!

WELL, YOU DID WRITE YOUR CHANUKAH LIST ON THE BACK OF YOUR *FATHER'S HEAD.*

LOOK, LIS! HE'S GOT PROACTIVE AND IN YOUR FACE *KUNG FU* ACTION!

BART, I HAVEN'T SEEN YOU WORK ON THE PAGEANT *AT ALL*...IT IS *TOMORROW MORNING*...

IT'S ALL *UP HERE,* LIS.

THE SEVENTH DAY OF CHANUKAH.

EXTRA, EXTRA! READ ALL ABOUT IT! MY BROTHER IS CHANGING HIS RELIGION FOR *GIFTS* AND *DAYS OFF!*

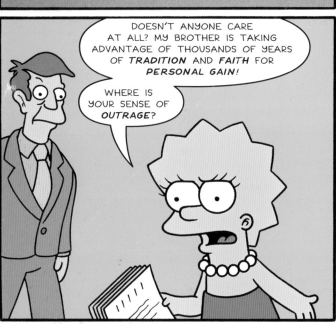

DOESN'T ANYONE CARE AT ALL? MY BROTHER IS TAKING ADVANTAGE OF THOUSANDS OF YEARS OF *TRADITION* AND *FAITH* FOR *PERSONAL GAIN!*

WHERE IS YOUR SENSE OF *OUTRAGE*?

PARDON THE INTERRUPTION OF LISA'S PATRONIZING DIATRIBE, CHILDREN, BUT I HAVE SOME *BAD NEWS*. DUE TO A SCHEDULING SNAFU, TATER TOTS WILL BE UNAVAILABLE FOR TODAY'S LUNCH.

FURTHERMORE, DUE TO A PRINTING ERROR, THEY WILL BE REPLACED NOT BY *FREEDOM FRIES*, BUT RATHER, *MORGAN FREEMAN* FRIES.

I AM OUTRAGED!

AS AM I!

C'MON, LIS, FEEL THE APATHY.

I'M CONVERTING TO CATHOLICISM FOR THE *FREE WINE*.

THAT NIGHT...

LISTEN, BUBIE, CAN'T WE SET OUR DIFFERENCES ASIDE AND PLAY WITH THE ITCHY AND SCRATCHY "DEATH, DEATH, REVOLUTION" INTERACTIVE PLAYSET?

BART, I THOUGHT WE FINALLY HAD *SOMETHING IN COMMON*. THAT WE FOLLOWED OUR HEARTS BECAUSE OF WHAT WE BELIEVE IN.

BUT, AS USUAL, THE ONLY THING YOU BELIEVE IN IS *SELF-GRATIFICATION*.

THE EIGHTH DAY OF HANUKAH.

KNOCK! KNOCK!

BART SIMPSON! COME IN, COME IN!

YOU'RE NOT GOING TO SLAM THE DOOR IN MY FACE?

ABSOLUTELY NOT. KENAHORA, I'VE NEVER SEEN A BOY OF YOUR AGE *SO COMMITTED* TO HIS SPIRITUAL LIFE.

YEAH, THAT'S ME. I AM *TOTALLY* COMMITTED TO MY SPIRITUAL LIE...I MEAN *LIFE!*

THE FIRST QUESTION I HAVE FOR YOU IS, DO YOU HAVE A FAMILY MEMBER THAT *SUPPORTS* YOU IN THIS DECISION, WHO DEEPLY *BELIEVES* IN YOU TAKING THIS STEP?

UM.

YES.

EXCELLENT! TO GET YOU STARTED, I WANT TO GIVE YOU A COPY OF "A TREASURY OF JEWISH HISTORY, HUMOR, AND FOOD-ORIENTED YIDDISH PHRASES."

UM...I ALREADY HAVE IT.

BART, ARE YOU OKAY?

NO, RABBI KRUSTOFSKI, I'M SERIOUSLY FARKLEMPT.

THIRTY MINUTES LATER...

...I'M GOING TO SAY THIS QUICKLY, SO IT'S LIKE TEARING OFF A BANDAID... YOUWERERIGHT.

SO, YOU'RE GOING TO CONVERT FOR *SPIRITUAL* REASONS, NOT JUST TOYS AND VACATION DAYS?

I'M NOT CONVERTING AT ALL, LIS. LOVE *THE RELIGION*, BUT, *OY*...I CAN'T HANDLE *THE GUILT*.

THE END

115

"IT BEGAN, AS MOST *FADS* DO, VIRTUALLY UNNOTICED. EARLIER THIS YEAR, THE *ITCHY AND SCRATCHY INTERACTIVE PLAYSETS* QUIETLY APPEARED ON TOYSHOP SHELVES, SIMPLY ONE MORE ADDITION TO AN ALREADY *BLOATED PRODUCT LINE*."

"LITTLE BY LITTLE, THE PLAYSETS BEGAN TO *SEEP* INTO *THE COLLECTIVE JUVENILE CONSCIOUS*; A BIRTHDAY PRESENT *HERE*, A GIFT FROM GRANDMA *THERE* AND SO ON. BY SPRING *VISIBILITY* WAS ON THE RISE AND A *GROUND SWELL* WAS TAKING HOLD."

"OF COURSE, THE INEVITABLE *MEDIA BLITZ* ONLY HELPED TO *SHARPEN DEMAND* AND KEPT THE TOYS *HOT SELLERS* THROUGH SUMMER."

"ONCE THE NEW SCHOOL YEAR BEGAN, THE ITCHY AND SCRATCHY CRAZE HAD SWOLLEN TO *EPIDEMIC PROPORTIONS*. THOSE CHILDREN WHO HAD HERETOFORE BEEN LACKING THESE *HOLY GRAILS OF TOYDOM* LOOKED ANXIOUSLY AHEAD TO THE COMING HOLIDAY SEASON. SURELY *THEN* THEIR *WISHES* WOULD BE GRANTED."

"ALAS, AS SO OFTEN HAPPENS WITH A FAD OF THIS NATURE, THE LARGE RETAIL OUTLETS HAD WOEFULLY *UNDERESTIMATED* YOUTHFUL DEMAND AND THE PLAYSETS WERE COMPLETELY *SOLD OUT* BY MID-NOVEMBER."

"WHICH BRINGS US TO THE PRESENT, 10:46 A.M. CHRISTMAS EVE, AND TO THE *ONLY PLACE* IN SPRINGFIELD WHERE THE *CHERISHED TOYS* MAY YET BE PURCHASED...."

OH, PLEASE. I AM ONLY *CHARGING THE GOING RATE*, PLUS A MODEST *MARK-UP* TO COVER *OPERATING EXPENSES*.

MODEST? THOSE PLAYSETS WERE SELLING AT TRY-N-SAVE FOR FIFTEEN DOLLARS!

WELL THEN, I SUGGEST YOU DO NOT DELAY AND *DASH* OVER THERE WITH THE SPEED OF *THE FLASH* HIMSELF!

OH, WAIT, WAIT! I REMEMBER! EVERY OTHER STORE IN TOWN IS *SOLD OUT*. SILLY ME.

...BUT THEN, THAT WAS THE *POINT* OF MY STORY, IF YOU HAD BEEN PAYING ATTENTION.

GEE, I DON'T MEAN TO BE A WHINY WILLIE, BUT COULDN'T YOU SEE YOUR WAY CLEAR TO GIVE US A TINY BREAK-AROONIE ON THE PRICE-AREENO?

IT IS CHRISTMAS, AFTER ALL...

ITCHY & SCRATCHY "Stoning the False Prophets Playset"

EXACT-AREENO! AND WITH THE CURRENT COMIC BOOK MARKET AS TORPID AS HAN SOLO IN CARBONITE, A SMALL BUSINESSMAN SUCH AS MYSELF DEPENDS ON THE HOLIDAYS FOR MAKING UP *LOST REVENUE*.

YOINK!

HOWEVER, AS A *SEASONAL BONUS*, I AM OFFERING ONE *FREE INTERACTIVE "POOCHIE"* FIGURE WITH EVERY ITCHY AND SCRATCHY PLAYSET SOLD.

IN YOUR FACE *DUDE-MEISTERS*... *NOT!*

PASS.

POOCHIE!

ICK!

NO THANKS.

WELL, THE TWINS WILL BE *CRUSHED* IF THEY DON'T GET THEM...

IT'S *THOUGHTFUL PARENTS* LIKE YOU THAT MAKE MY JOB A *CEASELESS JOY*.

IT REALLY WAS THE *ONLY* THING ON MILHOUSE'S LIST...

HMMMM!

"THEN *ITCHY THE GRITCH*, WITH HIS SLEIGH *LOADED DOWN*, DROVE TO THE TOP OF THE PEAK OUT OF TOWN."

HEE, HEE!

RUFF, RUFF, MAN.

"FROM *SCRATCHVILLE* HE'D STOLEN EVERY *LAST* GIFT AND TOY, THE CATS' CHRISTMAS FUN HE VOWED TO *DESTROY*"

"BEFORE ITCHY *DUMPED* EACH BOX, TREE, AND WREATH, HE TURNED FOR A LOOK BACK AT SCRATCHVILLE BENEATH. HE EXPECTED TO SEE THE CATS *WEEPING* AND *WAILING*..."

"...BUT INSTEAD THE GRITCH SAW HIS GRAND SCHEME *FAILING!*"

"EVERY CAT DOWN IN SCRATCHVILLE WAS *YOWLING* AWAY, IN *HAPPY CELEBRATION* OF CHRISTMAS DAY."

LA, LA, LA, LA, LAAAA!

"AND WHAT HAPPENED THEN? WELL, IN SCRATCHVILLE THEY SWEAR, ITCHY'S SMALL HEART *SWELLED* WITH GLEE THEN AND THERE."

AHH...

"WITH A SMILE IN HIS SOUL HE SPED DOWN THE MOUNTAIN..."

"...AND *CUT DOWN* SCRATCHY, WHO *GUSHED* LIKE A FOUNTAIN."

YAHHHHH!

HEH, HEH, HEH!

IT JUST GETS *BETTER* EVERY YEAR.

HA, HA!

125

HEY, KIDS! NOW YOU CAN REENACT *FAVORITE MOMENTS* FROM *THIS HEART-WARMING CLASSIC* WITH THE *NEW* "ITCHY AND SCRATCHY HOLIDAY" SET!

Holiday Playset

AAHHHH!

COOOOL!

MOM! GET READY TO ADD *ANOTHER PAGE* TO OUR CHRISTMAS LISTS!

HOMER, COULD YOU COME INTO THE KITCHEN, PLEASE?

IS THAT "COME INTO THE KITCHEN" LIKE, TO *EAT*, OR "COME INTO THE KITCHEN" LIKE, FOR *TALKING*?

TALKING.

OHHH...!

I DON'T KNOW WHAT TO DO, HOMIE. BART AND LISA BOTH WANT THOSE *NEW PLAYSETS* BUT THE DEALER AT THE COMIC BOOK STORE IS *CHARGING TOO MUCH* FOR THEM.

GRRR! ANOTHER *SHAMELESS PROFITEER* OUT TO MINE GOLD FROM *THE DREAMS OF INNOCENT CHILDREN!* WELL, THIS YEAR I'M NOT BUYING INTO IT!

WE'LL JUST *MAKE OUR OWN* CHRISTMAS PRESENTS! I'LL NEED PASTE, CONSTRUCTION PAPER AND ELBOW MACARONI! AND BRING ME GLITTER! MUST HAVE *GLITTER!*

ARE YOU SURE ABOUT THIS, HOMER?

I MEAN, IT'S A SWEET GESTURE, BUT I THINK THE DAY BEFORE CHRISTMAS IS A LITTLE *TOO LATE* TO START MAKING GIFTS FOR THE KIDS.

YOU'RE RIGHT, DAD.

GOOD. NOW COME BACK ME UP WHILE I *BEG LIKE A DOG*.

SORRY, WE'RE **CLOSED**

NO AND NO! FOR THE *LAST TIME,* THE PRICE ON THE PLAYSETS *STANDS* AS IS!

BUT NO ONE IN TOWN CAN PAY THAT MUCH!

YOU'RE PRICING YOURSELF OUT OF THE MARKET, MAN.

OH? WELL, I GUESS THE PARENTS WHO *TRULY* VALUE THEIR KIDS' HAPPINESS DON'T SEE IT THAT WAY. GOOD DAY.

YOU LOUSY...

THAT'S ENOUGH, BART!

WE DON'T HAVE TO TAKE HIS ABUSE! WE'LL BUY THOSE TOYS SOMEWHERE ELSE!

HA! TO FIND MORE PLAYSETS AT THIS HOUR WOULD THWART THE *DEDUCTIVE SKILLS* OF THE *DARK KNIGHT* HIMSELF!

THEN THAT'S JUST WHAT WE'LL DO! COME ON, *OLD CHUM!* TO THE *STATION WAGON!*

AH, THE *NAIVETE* OF THE TOY-UNENLIGHTENED.

I'LL PUT SEVERAL PLAYSETS ASIDE FOR WHEN YOU COME *CRAWLING BACK,*

ADDING ON MY TWENTY PERCENT *LAYAWAY FEE,* OF COURSE.

THERE ARE THOUSANDS OF CITIES IN AMERICA AND *SPRINGFIELD* IS ONE OF THEM!

WE'LL HIT EVERY DEPARTMENT, DISCOUNT AND TOY STORE IN THIS PART OF THE STATE! *SOMEONE'S* GOT TO HAVE THOSE PLAYSETS AT A *REASONABLE PRICE!*

YOU SAID IT, HOMER!

THE AUTOMATON'S TOWER, SHELBYVILLE.

EVERY PLACE ELSE IN TOWN IS SOLD OUT. NINETY BUCKS, FIRM!

BLAME IT ALL ON GABBO

THE CYBORG'S BASEMENT, OGDENVILLE.

NINETY-FIVE, TAKE IT OR LEAVE IT.

D'OH!

I MAKE FOR HOBBITS

$95 00

THE ROBOT'S PAGODA, NORTH HAVERBROOK.

D'OH!

SCRAM.

$100 00

I STILL SAY I COULD HAVE GRABBED THE SETS WHILE YOU *CLOCKED* THAT GUY WITH YOUR GRAMMY.

SPRINGFIELD 1 MILE

DAD, IT'S CHRISTMAS EVE, AND FOR ONCE I HAVE **MORE TOYS** THAN EVEN **I** COULD EVER WANT. SHOULDN'T WE THINK ABOUT GOING HOME?

NOT YET, BOY.

YOU SAW WHAT PEOPLE WILL PAY FOR THESE. WE'LL **SELL** OUR OVERSTOCK AND MAKE A MINT!

HOMER?

ITCHY AND SCRATCHY PLAYSETS $200.00 EACH

WHERE DID YOU GET ALL THESE TOYS?

WELL, THERE WAS THIS STALLED TRUCK AND...

CHECK IT OUT, LIS! DAD AND I ARE BREAKING INTO THE INSANELY **INFLATED** COLLECTIBLES MARKET!

OH, NOT THE SALVAGE LAW OF THE OPEN ROAD AGAIN!

NOW MARGE, THIS IS COMPLETELY UNLIKE **THE SUGAR INCIDENT!**

I'D THINK AFTER ALL YOU WENT THROUGH TO GET THESE, YOU MIGHT BE **SYMPATHETIC** TO KIDS IN THE SAME SITUATION.

YEAH, RIGHT. WHAT DO YOU WANT ME TO DO, **GIVE THESE AWAY** IN THE SPIRIT OF THE SEASON?

DID YOU SAY YOU'RE GIVING THOSE AWAY?

ITCHY SCRATCHY

HE SURE DID, RALPH.

YAY!

LISA!

YOINK!

THEY'RE HANDING OUT **FREE** PLAYSETS!

HOORAY FOR THE SIMPSONS!

HOW SWEET!

YOU'VE REALLY GOT THE HOLI-DIDDLY-DAY SPIRIT, HOMER!

UH, YEAH...

NO PUSHING, PLEASE. THERE'S PLENTY TO GO AROUND.

YOU **SAVED** MY KID'S CHRISTMAS!

SHUT UP, BOY! IF WE TRY TO CHARGE THEM NOW, THEY'LL RIP US TO BLOODY BITS!

DAD, THEY'RE TAKING **EVERYTHING!**

HEH! HERE YOU GO! HAPPY HOLIDAYS!

RIGHT. THAT IS THREE ITCHY AND SCRATCHY PLAYSETS AT EIGHTY DOLLARS PER, PLUS THE ADDITIONAL "DISMEMBERING TOOLS ACCESSORY KIT" AT TWENTY-NINE, NINETY-FIVE, PLUS...

AY! UN COSTO TAN TERRIBLE!*

(*SUCH A TERRIBLE EXPENSE!)

HEY, DON'T *WASTE* YOUR MONEY HERE! THE SIMPSONS ARE GIVING AWAY THE SAME TOYS FOR *FREE*!

ITCHY SCRATCHY
Itchy & Scratchy Land Figures

¿JUEGETES PARA GRATIS? AY, CHIHUAHUA!

YES WE'RE OPEN

NOW WILL THAT BE CASH, CHECK OR... HMMM?

WHAT'S *THIS*? EXPENSIVE COLLECTIBLES BEING GIVEN AWAY SANS FEE AND MARK-UP? SURELY I HAVE STUMBLED INTO AN EVIL MIRROR UNIVERSE OF *RODDENBERRYIAN* PROPORTIONS!

EXCUSE ME, YOU *CANNOT* DO THIS!

WHO SAYS?

507

ME! THE HONEST MERCHANT WHOSE TRADE YOU ARE *RUINING* WITH YOUR GROTESQUE DISPLAY OF LARGESS!

LOOK WHO'S TALKING, TUBBY!

HE MEANS THAT SINCE WE'RE GIVING AWAY OUR TOYS FOR NOTHING, HIS ARE NOW *WORTHLESS*.

135

WHY, FAT TONY! HAVE YOU COME TO LEAD US IN A *ROUSING CHORUS* OF "JINGLE BELLS"?

SADLY, NOT TONIGHT. WHAT WITH THE LEGITIMATE BUSINESSMAN'S SOCIAL CLUB HOLIDAY PARTY THIS EVENING, I AM AFRAID OUR VISIT MUST BE BRIEF.

WE WILL SIMPLY TAKE THE *TWENTY THOUSAND DOLLARS* YOU OWE US AND BE ON OUR WAY.

SURE. JUST LET ME GET MARGE'S PURSE AND...

TWENTY THOUSAND DOLLARS?!? I DON'T HAVE TWENTY THOUSAND DOLLARS!

REGRETTABLY, IT SEEMS WE WILL BE *RUNNING LATE* FOR THE PARTY AFTER ALL.

YOU SEE, HOMER, OF LATE THE BOYS AND I HAVE CUT BACK ON OUR INTERESTS IN CIGARETTE AND LIQUOR PROCUREMENT TO CONCENTRATE ON TOYS.

WITH THE COLLECTIBLE MARKET TAKIN' IN MONEY HAND OVER FIST, WE COULDN'T AFFORD NOT TO.

137

"BUT IMAGINE OUR *SURPRISE* WHEN WE RETURNED TO FIND ALL OUR CAREFUL MACHINATIONS *UNDONE*."

I KNEW I SHOULD HAVE TOLD ONE OF YOU GUYS TO WATCH THE TRUCK.

"WE FOLLOWED A PAIR OF *SUSPICIOUS* TIRE TRACKS INTO TOWN AND PROCEEDED TO ASK THE LOCALS IF THEY HAD SEEN ANYONE *FLASHING* A LARGE LOAD OF TOYS. THE GENTLEMAN AT THE COMIC BOOK STORE WAS *PARTICULARLY HELPFUL*."

YOU ARE HERE

1094 EVERGREEN TERRACE

I'LL *BET* HE WAS!

AS YOU CAN SEE, THOSE PLAYSETS WERE A *KEY PART* OF OUR END OF THE YEAR EARNINGS. WHILE I APPLAUD *YOUR ALTRUISTIC GESTURE* TO THE CHILDREN OF SPRINGFIELD, I MUST NOW INSIST ON *REMUNERATION*...

...OR *RETRIBUTION!*

URRRK!

HOMER!

CHILL, DOLL. I'LL HANDLE THIS.

JUST A SECOND, PATRON. REMEMBER ME? BART? YOUR *FAVORITE UNDER-AGE BARTENDER?* I'M SURE WE CAN WORK OUT A DEAL FOR *OLD TIME'S SAKE.*

SURE, BART. DO YOU HAVE TWENTY THOUSAND DOLLARS?

*EDITOR'S NOTE: BART TENDED BAR AT FAT TONY'S LEGITIMATE BUSINESSMAN'S CLUB IN "BART THE MURDERER", EPISODE 8F03 OF THE SIMPSONS TV SHOW.

WELL, NO, BUT...

HOW *DISILLUSIONING*. THERE REALLY *IS* NO HONOR AMONG THIEVES.

YEAH, BUT WHAT ARE YA GONNA DO?

WE FRAY THE CORD LIKE SO, PLUG IT IN, AND *VOOOM!* THE TREE GOES UP IN ONE NICE, NEAT FLASH.

IT'S A PLEASURE TO WATCH *THE MASTER AT WORK*, TONY.

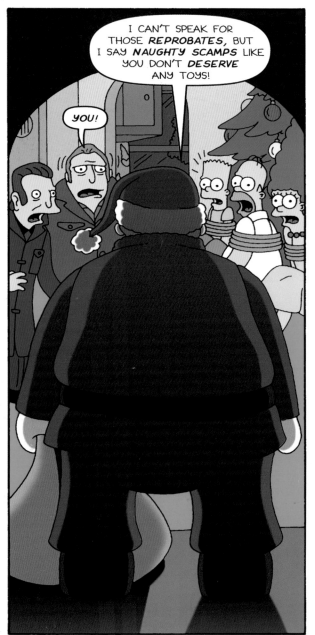

I CAN'T SPEAK FOR THOSE *REPROBATES*, BUT I SAY *NAUGHTY SCAMPS* LIKE YOU DON'T *DESERVE* ANY TOYS!

YOU!

ISN'T THERE SOME *OTHER WAY* TO SETTLE THIS?

I'M SORRY, MARGE. NOTHING PERSONAL, BUT *PROTOCOL* MUST BE SERVED. WHAT WOULD THE OTHER SPRINGFIELD DONS SAY IF THEY HEARD I *TOOK A BATH* IN THE TOY RACKET?

YES, IT IS *I*. AFTER YOU LEFT MY SHOP, I REALIZED THAT I HAD BEEN PERHAPS A TAD *OVERZEALOUS* IN MY DESIRE TO BRING *MISFORTUNE* ONTO THIS FAMILY.

DONUTS

TRUE. REVENGE IS AN *UGLY CYCLE*.

BUT THAT STILL DOES NOT CHANGE THE FACT THAT HOMER COST ME TWENTY G'S.

I AM AWARE OF THE DEBT. I HAVE COME BEARING *BARTER*.

DONUTS

BEHOLD. THE *MEGA-RARE ODDS MAKER PETE ROSE BASEBALL CARD,* THE *CROWN JEWEL* OF THE *COOPERSTOWN HALL OF SHAME* SERIES. *MINT CONDITION,* WORTH *TWENTY-FIVE THOUSAND* ANYWHERE. *YOURS* IF YOU LET THESE PEOPLE GO.

WHOOOA!

Pete Rose | ODDS MAKER

I HAVE BEEN LOOKING FOR *GAMBLING PETE* FOR YEARS. CUT THEM LOOSE, BOYS!

IN SPITE OF EVERYTHING, I'D STILL LIKE TO WISH YOU ALL A VERY HAPPY HOLIDAY SEASON.

NO HARD FEELINGS NOW.

IT'S *BUSINESS.* IT HAPPENS.

HOMER!

I GUESS WE OWE YOU A GREAT BIG THANKS, MR...

SAVE YOUR GRATITUDE. I DON'T MIND SAYING I HAD MY *OWN* WELL-BEING AT HEART MORE THAN YOURS.

THE TOY GIVE-AWAY THIS AFTERNOON TURNED YOU SIMPSONS, HOWEVER BRIEFLY, INTO *LOCAL HEROES*. IF IT CAME OUT THAT I HAD AIDED THE GANGSTERS, I WOULD HAVE BEEN FURTHER *VILIFIED* BY THE COMMUNITY, AND MY STORE *SHUNNED* LIKE A TREK FAN AT A B5 CONVENTION.

THAT IS *COLD*.

BUT PEOPLE HAVE *SHORT MEMORIES*, AND I AM *CONFIDENT* YOUR GOOD DEED WILL SOON BE *FORGOTTEN*. THEN I MAY ONCE AGAIN CHARGE AS I PLEASE FOR WHATEVER *FLASH IN THE PAN* TOY THAT NEXT SPARKS THE PUBLIC'S FANCY.

OOOH! NEW *FUNZO*!

HEY KIDS! NOW I'M MORE *FUNZO* THAN EVER! TEE-HEE!

MUST HAVE!

WELL, ALL THAT ASIDE, YOU *DID* SAVE OUR LIVES. WOULD YOU AT LEAST LIKE TO STAY FOR HOT CHOCOLATE AND COOKIES?

THANK YOU, NO. I AM LATE TO JOIN MY *FILKING GROUP*.

EACH CHRISTMAS EVE WE TRAVERSE SPRINGFIELD, *SUBSTITUTING* CLEVER SCI-FI *IN-JOKES* FOR THE LYRICS OF *WELL-KNOWN CAROLS*. "SULU HEAR WHAT I HEAR", "GOD REST YE MERRY X-MEN", "RUDOLPH, THE RED-NOSED ROMULAN", AND OF COURSE, THE EVER-POPULAR "WOOKIEE IN A WINTER WONDERL..."

UGGGGHHHHH!

SLAM!

ALL THINGS CONSIDERED, LIS', I'D SAY THIS WAS ONE OF OUR *BETTER* CHRISTMAS EVES. WE *MADE OUT LIKE BANDITS* AND NO ONE GOT *KILLED*.

YESSS, BUT I STILL HAVE THIS *NAGGING FEELING* THAT SOMETHING IS GOING UNRESOLVED.

COME ON, FELLAS, ENOUGH'S ENOUGH! GIL *NEEDS A BREAK* HERE, OKAY? FELLAS? YOU WOULDN'T LET OL' GIL DOWN, WOULD YA? *FELLAS*?

THE END